MEXICO

Written by Rod Barkman

COUNTRIES of the WORLD

PowerKiDS press

Published in 2025
by The Rosen Publishing Group, Inc.
2544 Clinton Street, Buffalo, NY 14224

Written by: Rod Barkman
Edited by: Elise Carraway
Designed by: Amelia Harris

Cataloging-in-Publication Data

Names: Barkman, Rod.
Title: Mexico / Rod Barkman.
Description: Buffalo, NY : PowerKids Press, 2025. | Series: Countries of the world | Includes glossary and index.
Identifiers: ISBN 9781499447217 (pbk.) | ISBN 9781499447224 (library bound) | ISBN 9781499447231 (ebook)
Subjects: LCSH: Mexico--Juvenile literature.
Classification: LCC F1208.5 B375 2025 | DDC 972--dc23

Manufactured in the United States of America
CPSIA Compliance Information: Batch #CSPK25. For further information contact Rosen Publishing at 1-800-237-9932.

Find us on

Image Credits
All images are courtesy of Shutterstock.com, unless otherwise specified. With thanks to Getty Images, Thinkstock Photo and iStockphoto. Cover – Kamira, lunamarina, David A Litman, Anna Kosheleva, GoodStudio. 2 – Rubi Rodriguez Martinez. 4–5 – Andrew Minsk, FrentaN. 6–7 – ecstk22, AlessandroV. 8–9 – Krakenimages.com, Cezary Wojtkowski. 10–11 – Monkey Business Images, clicksdemexico. 12–13 – Drazen Zigic, Digital Media Pro. 14–15 – Photostock by Leonardo Em, Nebojsa Markovic. 16–17 – antoniodiaz, Marcos Castillo. 18–19 – LightField Studios, Monkey Business Images. 20–21 – Pixel-Shot, Candice Bell. 22–23 – Kuryanovich Tatsiana, T photography.

CONTENTS

Words that look like <u>this</u> can be found in the glossary on page 24.

WHERE IS MEXICO?

Mexico is a country in the southern part of North America. The capital city of Mexico is called Mexico City.

The population in Mexico is over 128 million. Most people who live in Mexico speak Spanish.

LANDSCAPE AND WEATHER

Mexico has a hot climate all year round. In the dry season, there is hardly any rain and the ground gets very dry.

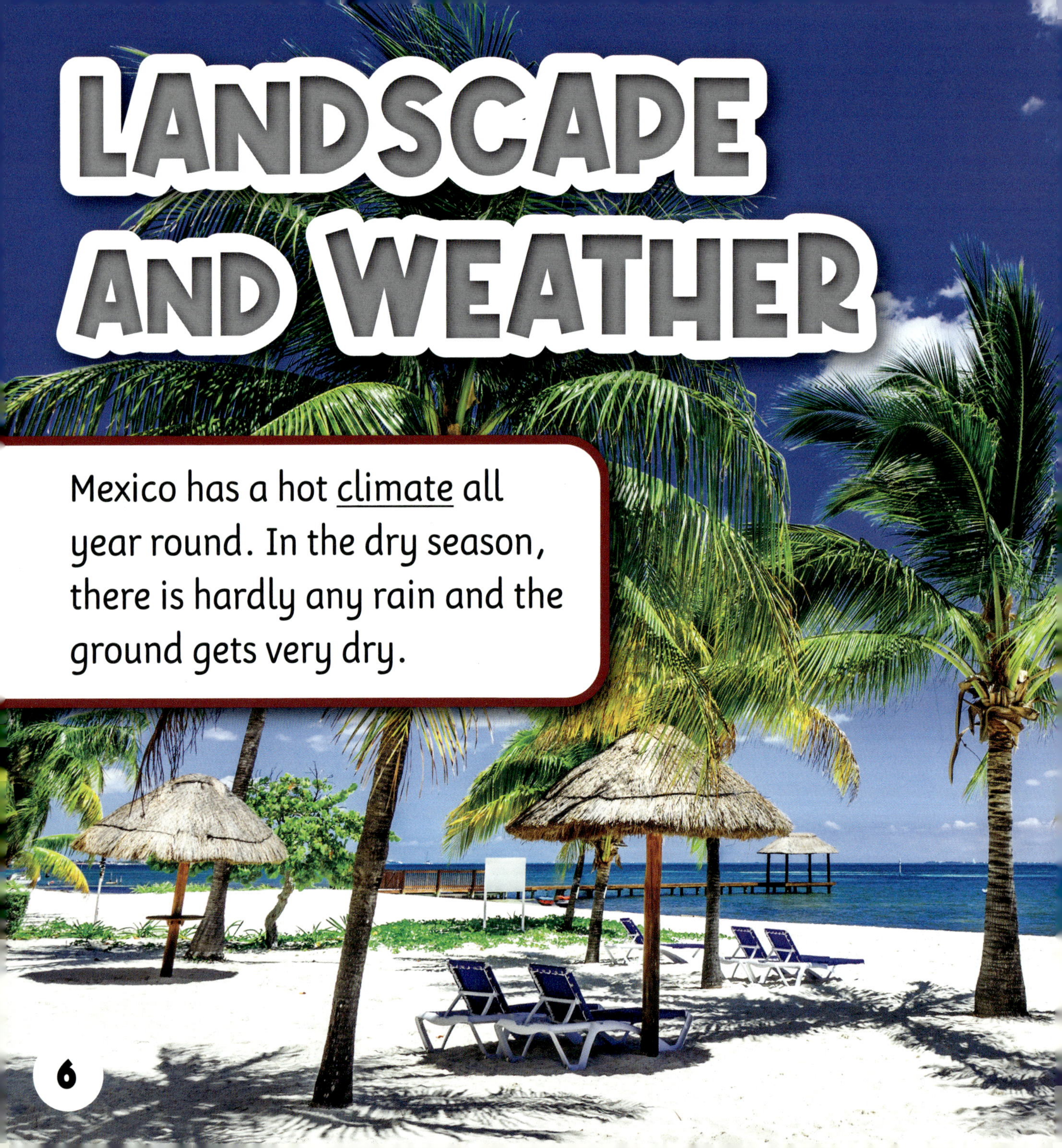

There are many different landscapes in Mexico. It has hot, sandy deserts and high mountains. Mexico also has long stretches of beach.

Sonoran Desert, Mexico

RELIGION

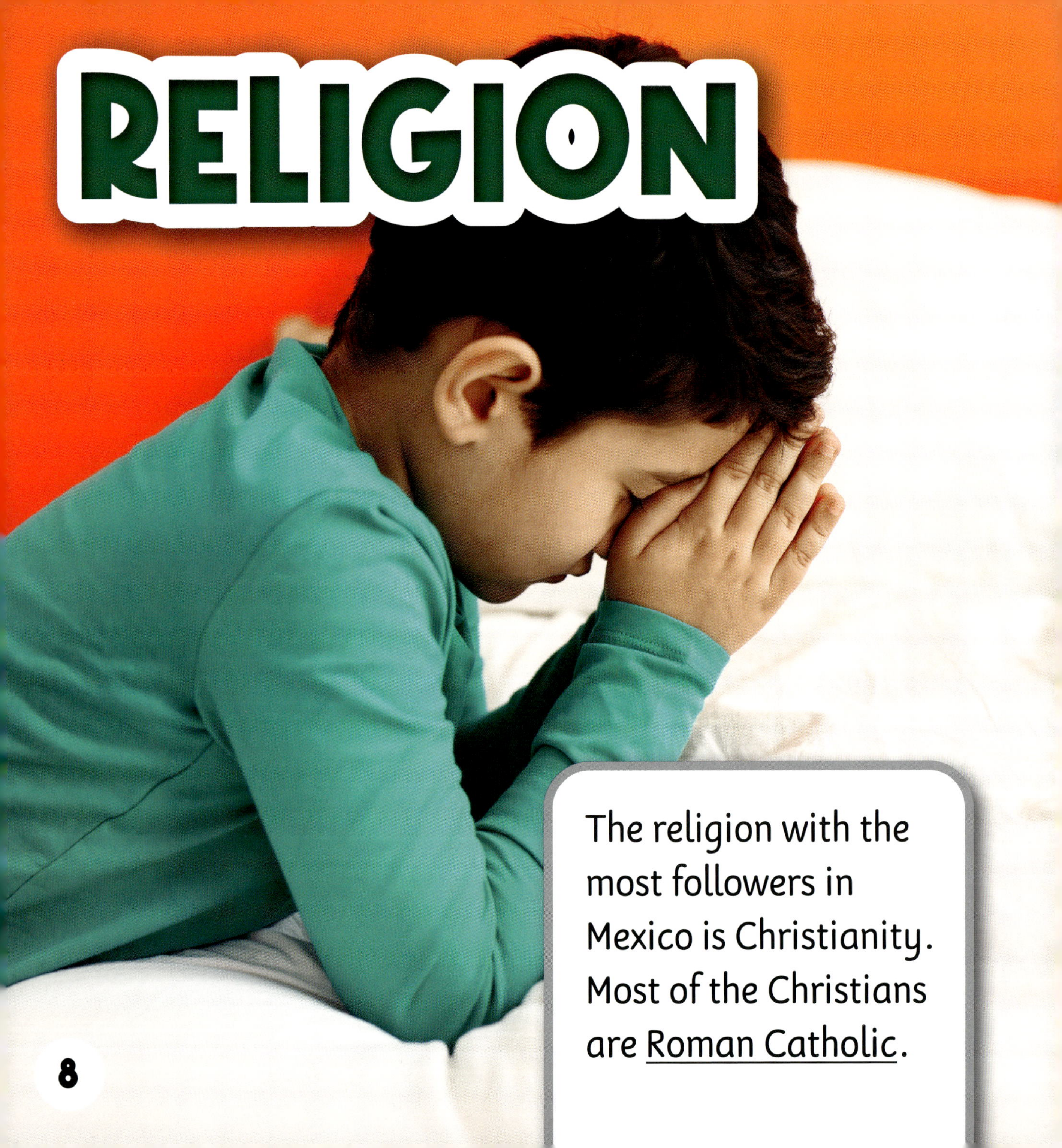

The religion with the most followers in Mexico is Christianity. Most of the Christians are Roman Catholic.

The Christian place of worship is a church. Many Christians visit churches every Sunday for prayer.

Basilica of Our Lady of Guadalupe, Mexico City

FAMILIES

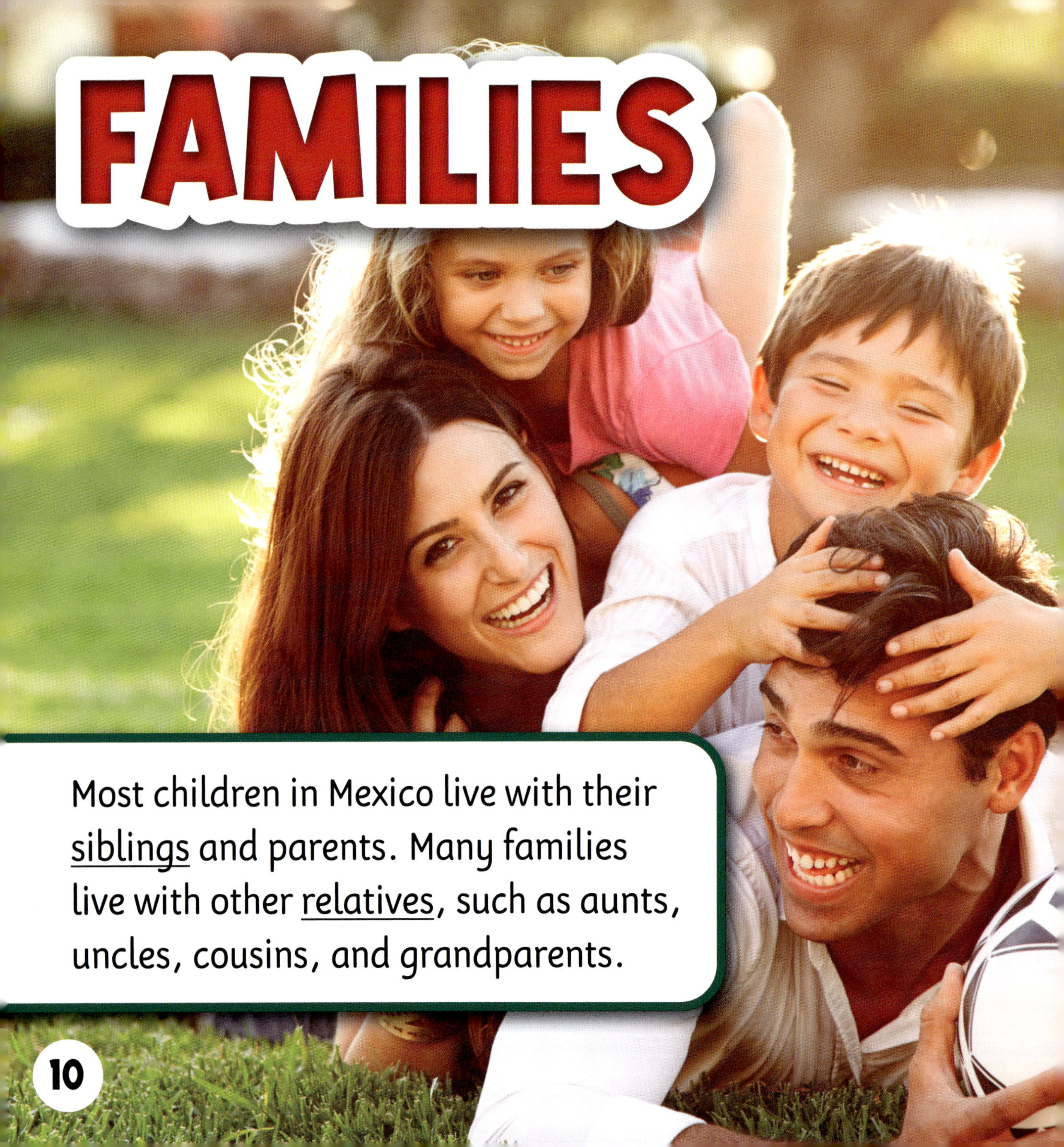

Most children in Mexico live with their siblings and parents. Many families live with other relatives, such as aunts, uncles, cousins, and grandparents.

Families like to come together to celebrate special occasions, such as birthdays. Children like to play the piñata game at parties.

Children take turns to hit the piñata to get to the sweets inside.

SCHOOL

Children who go to school in Mexico study Spanish, math, geography, science, and history.

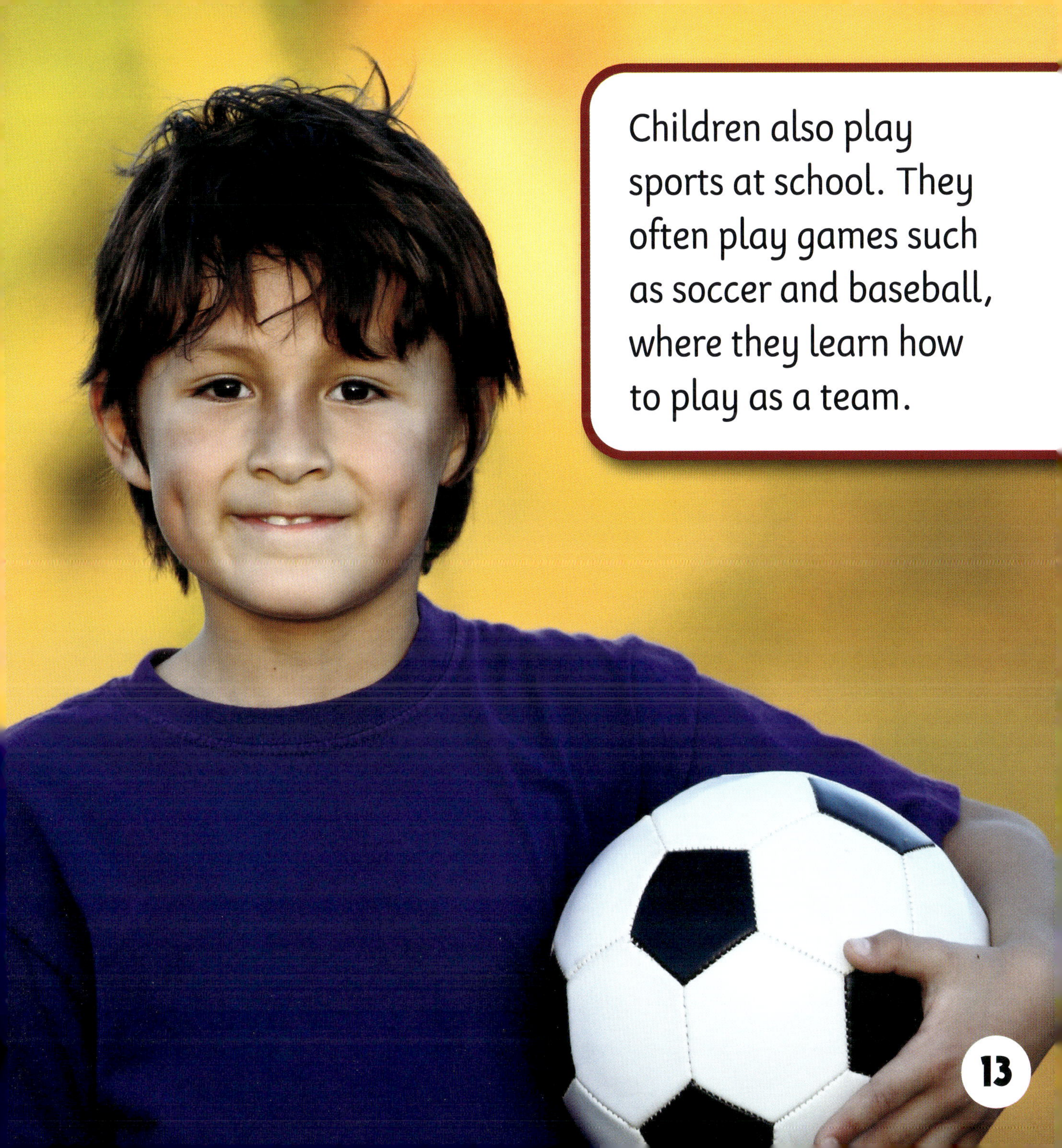

Children also play sports at school. They often play games such as soccer and baseball, where they learn how to play as a team.

HOME

In big cities in Mexico, many people live with their families in tall apartment buildings.

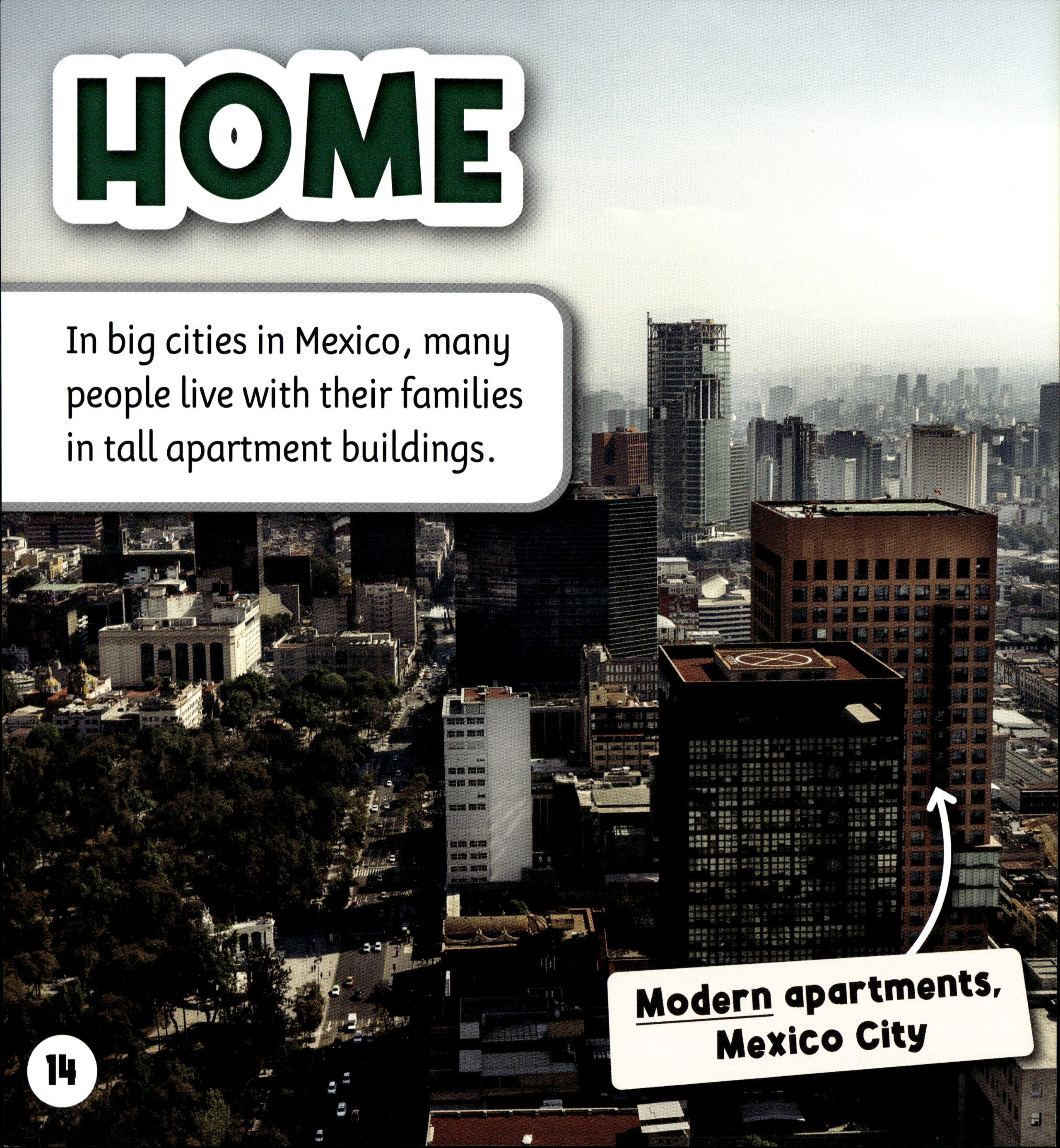

Modern apartments, Mexico City

Many families live on farms where they grow fruits and vegetables. Animals, such as donkeys, can also live on the farms.

CLOTHING

People in Mexico mostly wear cool and comfortable clothing because of the hot climate.

The sombrero is a traditional hat from Mexico. This is a very large hat that protects the head, neck, and shoulders from the sun.

SPORTS

The most popular sport in Mexico is soccer. Many children play soccer after school and watch their favorite teams on television.

Basketball is also a popular sport in Mexico. Two teams play against each other, and each team tries to throw a ball through one of the netted hoops.

FOOD

Mexican food can be very spicy. A well-known dish from Mexico is nachos. Nachos are made from tortilla chips and are often dipped in a spicy sauce called salsa.

Tortillas are very popular in Mexico. They are small pancakes made out of maize flour, and are often eaten with spicy food and sauces.

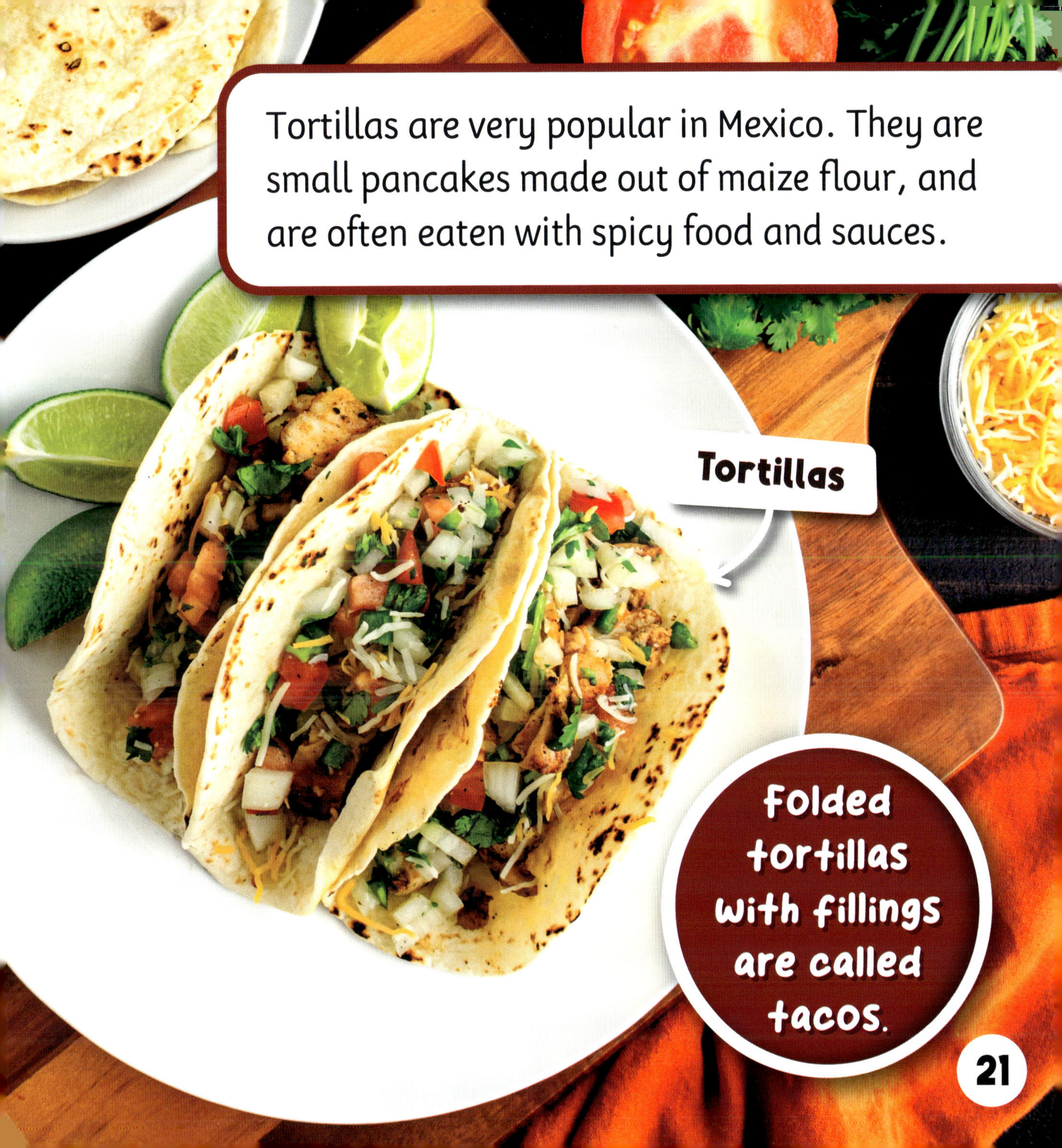

Folded tortillas with fillings are called tacos.

FUN FACTS

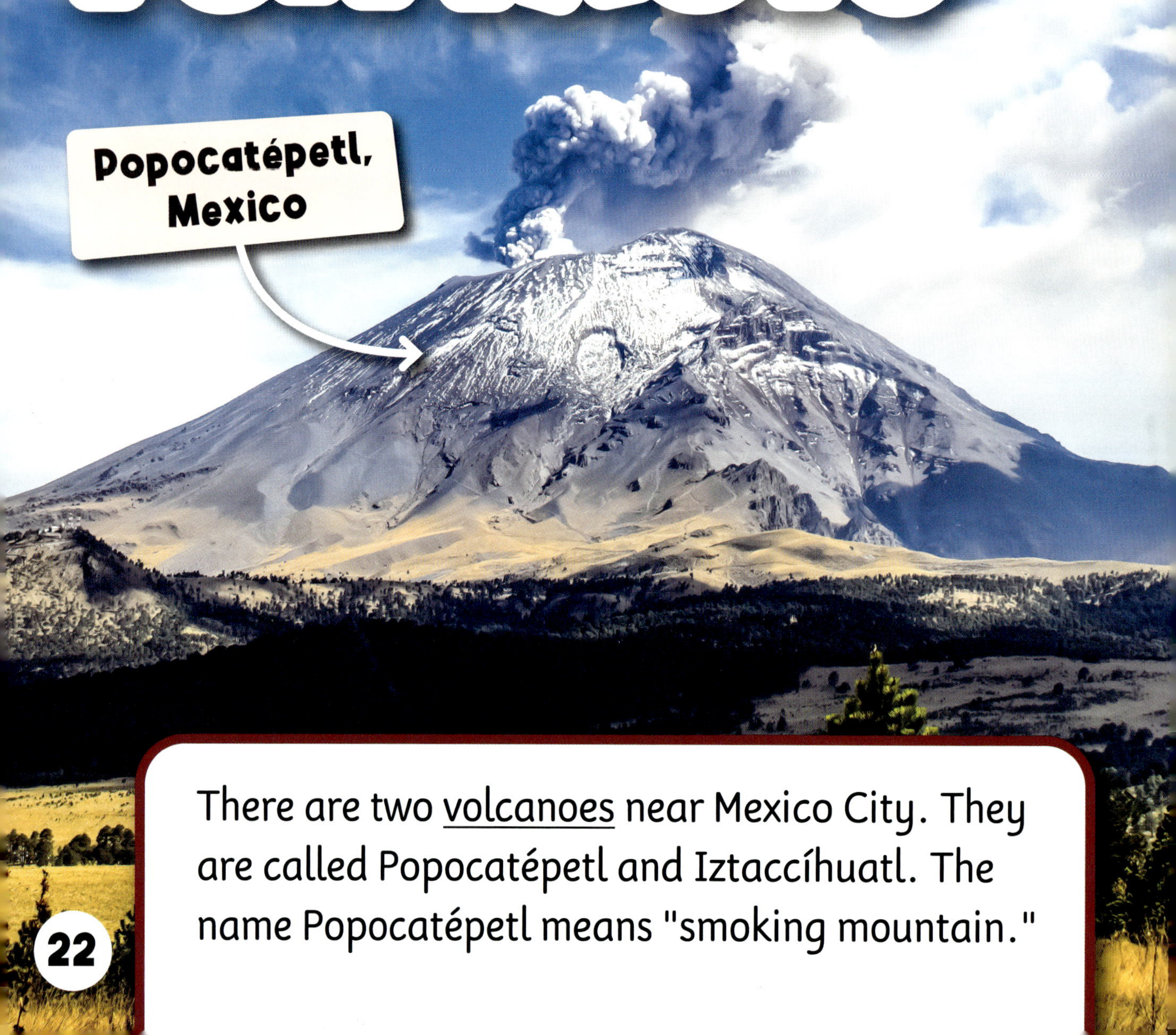

There are two volcanoes near Mexico City. They are called Popocatépetl and Iztaccíhuatl. The name Popocatépetl means "smoking mountain."

The longest river in Mexico is called Rio Grande. It is over 1,900 miles (3,058 km) long.

GLOSSARY

climate the weather in a large area

modern having to do with recent or present times

population the number of people living in a place

relatives different people in a family

Roman Catholic having to do with the type of Christianity that follows the beliefs of the Roman Catholic Church

siblings brothers and sisters

traditional having to do with beliefs, customs, or ways of behaving that have been around for a long time

volcanoes mountains that sometimes erupt, giving off very hot melted rock and gases

worship a religious act of praise, such as prayer

INDEX